Yes.

Yes.

Yes.

Yes.

Yes.

Yes.

Yes.

Yes.

Yes.

Yes.

Yes.

Yes.

Yes.

Yes.

Yes.

Yes.

Yes.

Yes.

Yes.

Yes.

Yes.

Yes.

Yes.

Yes.

Yes.

Yes.

Yes.

Yes.

Yes.

Yes.

Yes.

Yes.

Yes.

Yes.

Yes.

Yes.

Yes.

Yes.

Yes.

Yes.

Yes.

Yes.

Yes.

Yes.

Yes.

Yes.

Yes.

Yes.

Yes.

Yes.

Yes.

Yes.

Yes.

Yes.

Yes.

Yes.

Yes.

Yes.

Yes.

Yes.

Yes.

Yes.

Yes.

Yes.

Yes.

Yes.

Yes.

Yes.

Yes.

Yes.

Yes.

Yes.

Yes.

Yes.

Yes.

Yes.

Yes.

Yes.

Yes.

Yes.

Yes.

Yes.

Yes.

Yes.

Yes.

Yes.

Yes.

Yes.

Yes.

Yes.

Yes.

Yes.

Yes.

Yes.

Yes.

Yes.

Yes.

Yes.

Yes.

Yes.

Yes.

Yes.

Yes.

Yes.

Yes.